My Books

NON FICTION

How to Live with Bipolar
Bipolar 1 Disorder Rescue Plan
37 Symptoms of Bipolar Depression
The Bipolar Guide
A Practical Guide to Overcoming Loneliness
Get Well and Stay Well with Bipolar Disorder
Life Lessons

FICTION

Shards of Glass Series
Shards of Glass
Fragments of the Past
Memories Lost in Time

SHORT STORIES

One Summer
The Lucky Lady

POETRY

We Never Did Mornings

HUMOR

Funny Old Folk

GET WELL *AND* STAY WELL *WITH* BIPOLAR DISORDER

Lengthen the period between episodes

SALLY ALTER R.N.

Contents

Introduction

This book, unlike any other, is concerned with getting well and staying well with bipolar.

It is possible to get well, and many books have been written about that, but staying well is a different matter entirely. In this book, I want to discuss all the ways you can achieve remission and stay well for a long period of time even though you have this devastating illness. Wellness in between episodes is called the euthymic period when no or only a few symptoms are present. I want you to achieve wellness for a long time between episodes, and hope to make it possible in these pages.

To my knowledge, there is no other book like this on Amazon.

As bipolar is a cyclical illness, you cannot say you have been cured, but you can limit the number of recurrences and lengthen the frequency. That in itself, you will agree, is a huge relief. If you have suffered many symptoms for a long period of time, you will understand what I am talking about.

I went to a clinic for many years and their motto was **RECOVERY**. They used to talk about it all the time. Until one day I told the manager that you can never actually recover from bipolar, but you can go into remission. Since then, the clinic has dropped recovery from their vocabulary, and changed it to **REMISSION**. I think that is far more accurate.

Remission means having an absence or minimal symptoms of depression, mania, and mixed mood for at least a week.

I am an RN and have had bipolar since the age of 15. I am now 77, so you can see I have a wealth of experience. This is my fifth book on bipolar. After writing four books, I thought I had covered everything. Then I looked at my life, and realized I have achieved remission for the past four years, so there is still a lot to talk about. I want to share this knowledge with you.

I would like to do a time line for you (and me) so that you can see how bipolar has affected my life:

Age 15	Had my first manic episode. (My mother died when I was 15!)
Age 15 – 19	Well for 4 years.
Age 19 – 25	Constant depression. (Toxic living situations didn't help!)
Age 25	Diagnosed with bipolar disorder and given Lithium. Immediate mania when discontinued.
Age 25 – 28	Well for 3 years.
Age 28	Had my first psychotic episode and went to the hospital.

Age 28 – 47	Well for 19 years. (Had a full-time career in nursing. Traveled to many places in the world on Lithium.)
Age 47 – 73	Menopause and a return of my mood swings. Discontinued Lithium and tried about 25 different combinations of medications, all to no avail. Many depressions, manias and psychotic episodes. Many hospital admissions. (Husband committed suicide!)
Age 73	Stopped having episodes altogether. Complete remission on Vraylar and change of lifestyle. Wrote my first book.
Age 73 – 77	Well for 4 years.
Age 77	Still well and written 12 books.

I hope you could follow that time line – it is a very checkered history, isn't it? If you notice there were some long periods of remission that cannot be explained, except to say that I was taking Lithium and living with far less stress than before. Throughout my life, I have never discontinued my medication. I felt that, even though it was a rocky road, I was better off with medication than without. I never stopped trying to get well.

But even with medication I was very ill for 26 years during and after menopause. That was a very harrowing time, and I am glad it has passed. I had many years of illness, but have improved exponentially since I was first diagnosed in the 1970s. My life has gone through many traumas, but I am now happy and content in my retirement.

I don't know what age you are now, or how long you have had bipolar, but I am sure you found that time line interesting. You might like to create one for yourself.

This book covers the various symptoms of bipolar disorder (Depression, Mania etc.) It is divided into Triggers, Symptoms and an Action plan for each symptom. There are many lists of the things I do to remain well. You can try all these things for yourself, and add ones that are personal to you. There are blank pages throughout the book for your personal use.

I have not differentiated between getting well and staying well in this book because I have found that both these things require the same treatment. So if you do everything I suggest, you are likely to get well and stay well. That is my wish for you.

I have practiced most of the things in this book to maintain my wellness over the past four years, and hope you will do so also. Get well and stay well with bipolar.

I am rooting for you!

PART ONE

What is Bipolar Disorder?

Bipolar is a severe mood disorder that causes extreme shifts in mood from depression, mania or hypomania, and mixed episodes. It affects a person's behavior, thinking, and energy levels.

So what does this mean? Do you switch moods all the time? How does it affect your thinking? How do your moods change? What do you mean by a lack of energy? How does it affect your emotions?

We shall discuss all this and more in this book.

Bipolar begins when the person is in their late teens or early twenties. Sometimes, it is difficult to distinguish bipolar from hormonal mood changes in the adolescent years. But the mood swings in bipolar are far worse than those in puberty. And they are very disruptive to the person's school and home life. Then when a person starts working, this brings a new set of problems. It is difficult to hold down a job with bipolar. Some people have done it, and have a very successful career, but for others this is not possible.

A few people develop bipolar in their adult years, sometimes as late as in their 60s, but this is rare. Many of those people say they knew they had a problem all along, but they were either given the wrong diagnosis or no diagnosis at all. It is often a big relief when they find out they can do something about their mood swings.

Many people think a diagnosis of bipolar is a relief, whereas others think it is a stigma that they have to live with for the rest of their lives. There is still a lot of stigma attached to bipolar disorder even today when many people speak about it publicly.

Anosognosia is a separate diagnosis that describes people who don't believe they have bipolar. This is more prevalent than you might think. I for one, never realized I had bipolar for many years, even though I was in treatment, receiving therapy, and having many hospital admissions!

Bipolar is diagnosed when a psychiatrist, or other mental health professional, rules out physical causes and takes an exhaustive history. There are no blood tests or procedures that can prove bipolar exists. Most doctors think it affects the chemicals in the brain, but as yet, nothing has been proved.

There is also the question of who you should tell about your diagnosis. Some people never tell anyone, or a few chosen people, whereas others tell everybody who asks. I tend to think you should only tell people who have to know about it, like close relatives or bosses, otherwise people can take the diagnosis the wrong way because they have no understanding of it. I made a point of never telling anyone after losing all my relatives and friends to this illness. But when I started writing books about bipolar, I had to come out in the open about it! There is no one answer to this question. To tell or not to tell? It is a personal decision.

Types of Bipolar

Bipolar is divided up into four groups: bipolar 1, bipolar 2, cyclothymia, and bipolar NOS (not otherwise specified.) We shall only be talking about bipolar 1 and bipolar 2 in this book as these two variations of the illness cause the most disruption in a person's life. Bipolar 2 is not a simpler version of bipolar 1, it has its own diagnosis.

- ★ A diagnosis of bipolar 1 is given when the person has had at least one manic episode lasting a week or needing hospital intervention. Depressive episodes are not necessary for this diagnosis although most people with bipolar 1 have depression at some time during the course of their illness.

- ★ A diagnosis of bipolar 2 is given when a person has had at least one hypomanic episode and one major depressive episode. Some people with bipolar 2 claim that their depressions are worse and last longer than people with bipolar 1, but of course depression is a personal experience and cannot be quantified.

Psychosis is possible in bipolar 1 disorder, in either the depressive or manic mood. This usually requires hospitalization. People with bipolar 2, or major depressive disorder, can have psychosis with a very severe depressive episode.

Cause of Bipolar

Like many other mental illnesses, nobody knows the cause of bipolar. Many people say it is caused by an imbalance of chemicals in the brain, but if that were the case, all the people who are given mood stabilizers would be well. Nevertheless, psychiatrists continue to treat bipolar with medications in the hope that they will find a combination that works.

The next theory is that it is genetic, and while there is definitely a preponderance of bipolar in some families, other families have had no experience with mental illness at all.

And the same goes for the third theory – some say it is caused by childhood trauma. This is sometimes the case in severe abuse and toxic living conditions, but not all children who have suffered abuse get bipolar. Losing a parent or even two parents in childhood is also thought to be a cause of bipolar. This applies to me as both my parents died before I was 15. I would say this is the cause of my illness, yet again, nothing has been proved.

Until somebody comes up with a definite cause for bipolar, we are left with what we know about this illness. Sadly, there is no known cure either. Many things have been tried but nothing works. More scientific study needs to be done on bipolar.

Treatment

Medicines certainly help a lot of people, I would say the vast majority of people, so they are very important as a first line of defense. But even with medication, therapy, and a stress-free life situation, bipolar keeps coming back. People who take medications that work for them are to be envied by many sufferers of this horrible illness.

Some people stop taking medicine to help the symptoms of bipolar, and this is fine if they can control the illness with other methods, but most people who stop taking their medications have to go back on it at higher doses, or take a different medication altogether as the symptoms will probably return worse than before. Many people will have a hospital admission as well.

It is a chance some people are willing to take. But many people, who have tried to quit a number of times, finally realize that it does take medication as well as a healthy lifestyle to control this illness.

Then there are the people who can't take medicine for one reason or other. Usually it is because of severe side effects. When you put on 50lbs in three months with some anti-psychotics, or have extreme headaches and your hair falls out with some mood-stabilizers, it is certainly disappointing, and causes people to give up on taking medications altogether. However, other people can see the benefit of taking medication regardless of the side effects. This should be a decision that is reached by you and your doctor.

Not all side effects are impossible to live with, though, and most are mild. These normally go away in a couple of weeks. I was lucky and have never had side effects from most medications. You have to remember that all medicines, even Aspirin, have side effects, so it takes the body a while to adjust. But in the end, you are in control of your medications. A therapist once told me, you must consider what you want to put into your body. And she was right.

For most people, medicines are the best way of keeping the illness in check. It can take a period of months, even years, to get the balance right, but if you persevere, you and your doctor are likely to find a cocktail that will work for you.

The way I look at it this. There are many diseases that are very serious like bipolar, and all of those diseases require medicines to make life worth living or to keep the person alive. I can think of many illnesses off the top of my head; high blood pressure, diabetes, thyroid disease, kidney and liver disease, cancer, epilepsy, and so on. Some of these illnesses can be fatal if medicines are not taken. And so it is with bipolar. It has an extremely high suicide rate.

Personally, I have to take 10 medicines a day for the rest of my life. It is annoying and inconvenient, but if I want to stay alive then I must take them. Six of those medicines are for bipolar, the rest are for various illnesses I have accumulated the older I have gotten.

It is true I have had some medicines that didn't agree with me, or had no effect on my illness, but getting the balance right can take a long time and lots of patience. I have finally found a medicine that works for me, and with therapy and a healthy lifestyle it has kept me well for the past four years.

I take these medicines, one by one, and say to myself, “I'm glad some scientist invented this medicine to keep me well!” You may not want to go that far, but I hope you will give medicines a try.

As with everything else about bipolar, it is a personal choice whether to take medicines or not.

It is advised that a person should have some form of therapy along with a medical regime as this can help stabilize your everyday problems. Cognitive Behavioral Therapy, talk therapy, group therapy or family therapy are some of the therapies available. You will have to see what is available in your area.

This is ideal, of course, but always possible for a number of reasons.

A change in lifestyle may well help your bipolar. It is very important to get enough sleep, eat a healthy diet and get some exercise.

Course of the Illness

People with bipolar can have very erratic mood swings as seen in my timeline in the introduction. You can be well for long periods of time before the mood changes. Some people are lucky in that they can go months to years without an episode, but for most people, the episodes are more frequent.

Some people have long bouts of depression and/or mania, whereas others can be sick for a short time. Nothing is written in stone with bipolar. Something that many people have noticed is that the mood can change instantly from mania to depression. This is alarming and can make a person very ill indeed. It is fair to say that bipolar is a difficult illness to live with. It is no wonder the average person has no understanding of bipolar. Even if you have it yourself, it is still not easy to understand. That is why I recommend educating yourself and those who are supporting you. There is a lot of information in the library, online and in books. I have written five books on bipolar, and they are all for sale on Amazon.

Mixed states where the symptoms of depression and mania appear at the same time are quite common, especially in bipolar 1. And rapid cycling occurs when episodes are daily, weekly, or monthly in a four month period. It is possible to have episodes that change within a day, or even an hour. This is very disruptive to a person's life.

As I have pointed out, bipolar is a cyclical disorder. This means it can affect you with the change of seasons. Some people have depression in the winter months and mania in the summer. An ultraviolet lamp – 10,000 lux – can be of help with depression. You could sit under it every morning for 30 or 60 minutes when you wake up. You can buy these lamps on Amazon.

Mood swings may increase when the body is going through a hormonal change as in puberty, pregnancy, or menopause.

Living with Bipolar

Bipolar has a nasty habit of ruining all your relationships, your education, your work life and your finances. Not to mention the disruption it causes in your way of thinking. When you think you will never get well again, it is difficult to come out of an episode.

Bipolar is like living on a roller coaster. If you have rapid cycling, you never know from one minute to the next what mood you will be in. The moods are not like the ordinary ups and downs that most people experience in life, they are more severe, and uncontrollable. They usually go on for much longer, as well.

Depression brings with it feelings of sadness, hopelessness, guilt, and suicidal thinking. Some people get very ill with depression and have to go to the hospital. Mania/hypomania, on the other hand makes the person elated or irritable. Sometimes, because the mood is elevated, they do not think they are ill so it is difficult to get them to agree to go to the hospital. People with bipolar 2 rarely have to go to the hospital.

As well as the changes in mood, many people with bipolar 1 also experience psychosis at some point in the illness. Psychosis means having hallucinations or delusions like people with schizophrenia. It can be difficult to differentiate between bipolar and schizophrenia, but people with bipolar 1 may only have temporary psychosis when they are experiencing extreme episodes of mania or depression. If psychosis occurs in bipolar 2, the person may get a new diagnosis.

From talking with other people who have bipolar, I have found that mood swings are not the only symptoms of bipolar. This applies to me, and may very well apply to you. Bipolar also brings about physical symptoms, especially with certain medications, such as thyroid disease, high blood pressure, heart problems, and kidney and liver disease. These are serious illnesses, and you would be wise to visit your doctor for annual check ups just to make sure you are staying healthy. Certain medications require regular blood tests, so never skimp on these.

I have also found that some people experience minor symptoms between episodes which I call bipolar 'blips.' I have had many of these blips in the past and they are most embarrassing. They involve saying and doing stupid things in public, things that embarrass yourself and others. I have never read anything about these blips in any publication on bipolar, but have found they are very real. This may apply to you as well.

Then there are the other illnesses that seem to occur with bipolar disorder like PTSD, obsessive compulsive disorder, borderline personality disorder, anxiety, anxiety attacks, panic attacks, insomnia, eating disorders, and rage. These can be very disturbing indeed, and often require treatment. There is also a correlation between bipolar and abuse of alcohol and/ or street drugs. This is called dual-diagnosis and is difficult to come to terms with. Treatment can involve intervention by several different professionals.

There is some debate as to whether bipolar 1 mania or bipolar 2 hypomania is worse. They have the same symptoms, and cause a disruption in people's lives. However, people who have hypomania report that they are sometimes very productive and creative. On the other hand, people with bipolar 1 find that mania can quickly escalate out of control, and the risks involved with the illness can make a productive life impossible. As I have said before, there is also the risk of psychosis with bipolar 1.

Major depressive disorder is similar in that the depressions are equally as bad, but major depressive disorder is a unipolar illness so there are no manic or hypomanic mood swings.

Bipolar is a cyclical disorder which means you may have long periods of remission, but as there is no cure, you will likely get more episodes in the future. This can be very frightening. But if you follow the advice given in this book, I hope you will have fewer and less severe mood swings in the future.

There hasn't been enough research done yet, but it has been said that bipolar symptoms worsen with age. Since finding a good medication regimen, my manias and my depressions have disappeared.

Now that I have been free of symptoms for 4 years, I wonder when it will rear its ugly head again. This is my chance to do all the things I have outlined for you in this book.

PART TWO

Healthy Lifestyle

There are so many things to worry about in the treatment of bipolar disorder, but a healthy lifestyle, along with medication and therapy, are the way to go if you want to minimize or eliminate episodes altogether.

This section covers the things you can do every day to help manage your bipolar. Sleep is of great importance in bipolar, as is diet and exercise, so we shall talk about them here. And in addition I have covered a daily routine and journaling which I have found very helpful indeed.

Bipolar is difficult to live with, as you know, and even harder to manage, but if you are diligent and keep up with a healthy life style, you are likely to be successful in keeping episodes away.

Sleep

Sleep is of the utmost importance in the treatment of bipolar. Many, if not most people with bipolar, have some form of sleep dysfunction. Sleep becomes difficult to achieve in many cases of depression and people often suffer from chronic insomnia. On the other hand, deep depression can cause too much sleep (hypersomnia) where the person sleeps for 16 or even 18 hours a day. It is very difficult to wake them, and difficult for them to stay awake except for a few minutes each day.

Mania/hypomania also causes sleep problems. People with mania often can't sleep for more than about 2 to 3 hours a night. Some never sleep at all. In fact, if you find you cannot sleep for a couple of nights, it can lead to a manic episode. If you notice any symptoms do call your doctor.

To get a good night's sleep it may be helpful to follow the same regime every night. A routine for sleep is important. It is also important to have the same environment for a good night's sleep.

Here are some things you can do:

- ☐ Go to bed and wake up at the same time every day
- ☐ Play some relaxing music or listen to an audio book.
- ☐ Do not exercise before bed.
- ☐ Keep the bedroom dark.
- ☐ Do not look at an LED screen an hour before bed
- ☐ Keep the bedroom for sleep and sex only.
- ☐ Keep the bedroom cool.
- ☐ Read something light.
- ☐ Do not drink coffee or alcohol before bed.
- ☐ Turn off all devises.
- ☐ Do relaxation or muscle relaxation exercises.
- ☐ Keep the bedroom quiet.
- ☐ Do visualization exercises.

Diet

It is always good to eat a healthy diet, but more important than ever if you have bipolar.

Pay attention to what you eat every day. You can even keep a food diary to check to see if you are eating healthy foods. Cut down on sweet and salty foods, especially if you have kidney disease or high blood pressure. Cook without salt as well.

Eat plenty of fruits and vegetables, grains and lean meats.

Shop on the periphery of the store. Go down the isles for things like pasta and olive oil. You may find fresh food is more expensive, but it will do your more good than buying processed food. Also processed foods have a lot of sugar and salt in them.

If you want to limit what you eat, you may find using a smaller plate helpful. Eat 2/3 of the amount of meat you would usually eat, especially if it is red meat. Fill yourself up on fruits and vegetables. Drink plenty of water.

You may find some medications (especially anti-psychotics) make you put on weight so you will need to discuss this with your doctor. Sometimes you may both come to the conclusion that it is better to carry a bit more weight and be well. But that is a personal decision.

Some people lose a lot of weight with depression. This should be discussed with your doctor.

Here are some foods that will help you get well and stay well with bipolar:

Whole Grains	Whole grain bread
	Oatmeal
	Whole grain pasta
	Brown rice
	Quinoa
OMEGA-3 fatty acids	Salmon
	Tuna
	Trout
	Sardines
	Eggs
Turkey	
Beans	Black beans
	Chick peas
	Lentils
Nuts	Peanuts
	Almonds
	Cashews
Probiotics	Yogurt
	Kefir
	Miso
Herbal Teas	
Dark Chocolate	
Saffron	

Exercise

Sleep, diet and exercise are the usual pieces of advice to keep well with bipolar, and I can vouch for that. I have not had a single symptom of bipolar since starting an exercise routine at the gym three years ago. I feel really fit and healthy even for a 77 year old. In fact, I am the youngest person at the gym as it is attached to the local hospital and physical therapy department.

Exercise is great for the body and mind, and particularly helpful to keep bipolar symptoms at bay.

You will find that exercise is good for depression and mild hypomanias as it releases endorphins, the brain's "feel good" chemical. It also elevates your mood and helps you sleep better. It is not advised for people in a manic episode because it can worsen the symptoms.

Do try things that make you feel good. You may not like walking around the mall, but you may like swimming in the town pool. If you go to the gym, you will feel amazing, but get proper training before you begin. Make exercise a daily habit. Twenty minutes a day is a great start. You can work up to forty minutes as you get stronger.

I also think it is a good idea to lift weights, even or especially if you are a woman. This will make your arms and your chest strong. Be warned not to strain yourself, though, as this can do more harm than good.

Many people try yoga and qi gong as these are good for balance and relaxation of the mind. I have discussed this in detail in my book "Bipolar 1 Disorder Rescue Plan."

You may like to keep an exercise diary so that you can keep track of the exercises you are doing. If you have not exercised before, see your doctor first. Start slowly and work you way up. Vary your exercise so that it is fun to do.

Team sports is a great way to get exercise. Play tennis, basketball or football with your friends. Get out in the sunshine and get all that good vitamin D!

Also, study mindfulness as this is sure to bring you peace.

Routine

It is a fact that people with bipolar have a hard time sticking to a routine. It is not clear why this is so, except to say that when you are in a manic mood you may find it difficult to come down to earth. And when you are in a depressed mood you have no energy to do anything, let alone work on your routine. That is just the way it is. The best way to get into a routine is to set it up when you are feeling well and stick to it. A good routine will help you get well and stay well. Perseverance is the name of the game.

A routine and a schedule are often talked about interchangeably, but I think they are different. A routine is what you do every day, whereas a schedule is a note of appointments you must go to. If you want to keep up with a schedule, you would be advised to buy a schedule book and write everything down so you don't forget where you are supposed to be on a certain day at a certain time. If you have appointments with doctors, it is essential that you remember them, so writing the appointment down will help you remember. You can also use an app on your phone, or an online scheduler.

Personally, I use a planner to help me remember appointments. I write all kinds of things in my planner, but when I write an appointment down, I highlight it in yellow which tells me at a glance that I have to go out somewhere and must be there on time.

On the other hand, a routine requires structure which is often difficult for a person with bipolar to achieve. I had no idea how to structure my life for years, and every day was spent in chaos. I went from one thing to the next without a thought, and this did not work out for me. I would repeat things or forget to do them altogether. I remember I once told a woman that I lived in chaos, and she gave me a very strange look, but I didn't know any other way to live.

I had a case worker at my clinic who spent many weeks trying to teach me how to apply a routine to my life. It was like climbing a mountain, I just couldn't get to the top. I can't say I suddenly had an "Ah! Ha!" moment. I just learned to adjust. If you have a problem with routine, you can adjust, too. It may take some time, but do persevere and make it happen. Of course, it is difficult to stick to a routine when you have depression or mania, but do persist.

I suggest you write your routine down on paper. You might like to use a sticky note that you can put on your bathroom mirror. That way, when you are brushing your teeth in the morning, you won't forget what you have to do next. Otherwise, you can make a note and stick it on the fridge. Try anything that will help you remember your routine.

Also, do take your time. If you make your routine too rushed you will get exhausted and give up too soon. Seeing as I have had a routine for years, I know it by heart and don't need to time myself.

I think the best way to talk about a routine is to show you mine. That way you will be able to adjust it to your way of life. The first thing you will need to decide on is what time to get up in the morning. This is important. If you can stick to a regular bedtime and wake time, you will be half way towards achieving your goal. Lying in bed for any amount of time will make it difficult to start on your morning routine, and you will find yourself rushing to catch up.

I have worked on my routine for so many years now that I no longer need a reminder. And most things roll into one. The times are just a guide. You will be able to make your own times.

My routine:

9:00
- Get up and make the bed
- Feed my cat, Greta
- Brush my teeth

9:30
- Make a pot of coffee

9:35
- Take my thyroid tablet

9:40
- Do my emails and Facebook
- Take a shower and get dressed
- Eat breakfast

11:00
- Take the rest of my morning tablets
- Journal

Noon
- Deep breathing exercises

13:00
- Start my day

Do make a big effort to write down your routine and stick to it.

Another thing that may help you is to regulate your meal times. You are already regulating your sleep, so when you have regular meal times you set your body clock for the next 24 hours. This is called your circadian rhythm. It is like a pacemaker in your brain. If you can get your body clock working for you, you will be doing very well.

(I also have a 'tummy clock' which goes off in my mind when I am full. Then I stop eating.!!!)

A routine helps you gain control of your life. If you have experienced a traumatic incident, stick to your routine then you will feel more in control.

Take note of rumination as well. Many people with bipolar spend a lot of time ruminating which upsets their routine. Do you do it? Rumination means thinking the same thoughts over and over again – they run through your mind like a film that is non-ending. And of course, the thoughts are never good. You criticize yourself for everything you do. It is a running commentary. But criticizing does no good. It only makes you miserable if you aren't already. The answer is compassion. Be nice to yourself. Take care of yourself like nobody else can. As I say, if you don't take care of yourself, nobody is going to do it for you.

Also, think about making time for fun in your routine. A nurse at the clinic asked me once what I did for fun, and I looked at her aghast. Fun! It hadn't crossed my mind that I should be having fun and enjoying my life. I really had to dredge up something I could do that might be fun. I am an artist, so I thought that might be fun to do again seeing as I hadn't picked up a paint brush in years. I made time for painting and it lifted my mood. I am sure you have things you can do for fun. You may have forgotten all about them, but it is never too late to start again.

Make sure your to-do list is not overwhelming. We all have lots of things we need to do, but you can't do them all in one go. I generally do three things in one day. No more. That is quite enough. If I go out, I do three errands, and if I stay at home, I do three chores in one day. You need balance in your life.

When I used to be severely depressed, I only did one thing in a day. I put the laundry in the machine. Then the next day, if I was feeling up to it, I put it in the dryer. A doctor told me to do that once, and I thought she was uncaring because I was too ill to do that, but I tried it for myself and it worked. I finally got better and could do more things.

If you should have to go into the hospital, you will notice immediately that they have a strict routine. You always know what will happen next: breakfast at 7, medications at 9, lunch at noon, snacks at 3, evening meal at 7, and last medications of the day at 9. Like clockwork. With that kind of structure, you will always feel good about yourself. Routines make you feel cared for.

Sadly, when many people are discharged from the hospital,

they are at a loss because they no longer have a routine. This is when it is good to have your routine written out on a sheet of paper or a sticky note, then you can catch up to where you left off.

Journaling

If you look in my deep desk drawer you will find dozens of journals. I love journaling, and find it really helps to keep me well. I am sure it would help you as well. Do you journal? It is a wonderful way to express yourself. Try it.

There are many different ways to journal. You will find apps on your phone, or you can open a document on your computer and journal in that. I prefer the old fashioned way of using journals you buy from the store or online. It is amazing how many beautiful journals there are these days. I like to get a pretty journal and a nice pen that writes well. In 2015, I started a journal on my computer desktop and worked with it for some years. It got me through some tough times, but I much prefer to write in my journal now.

But what do you write in your journal? Do you have enough to talk about? Believe me, you have. You can journal your thoughts, feelings and behaviors – the things that affect people with bipolar. You can also journal your personal goals, the events that take place in your life, and your reactions to them.

If you want to use it as a Gratitude Journal do so. Or you can use a separate journal for that. We have a lot to be grateful for. If you can find five things a day, you will start to see a change in your mood.

Many people use a journal for stream of consciousness writing where they write whatever comes into their minds. This is a therapeutic way to journal. Do not judge yourself, just write. Thoughts will pop into your head. Write them down. Thoughts are neither good nor bad. I think of them as clouds passing by in the sky. You can watch them change, but you never judge them.

One thing that is great to journal, and would help you in your everyday life, is working on your emotions. You will find that thoughts influence your emotions (feelings) and your feelings influence your behavior. Not the other way around. If you think something is good, you will feel good, but if you think something bad, you will feel bad. And this in turn will affect your behavior. Thinking badly about yourself will cause guilt, shame, and depression. And with bipolar, we know we don't want that.

So what you think is very important.

People with bipolar often criticize themselves. They criticize themselves about everything. This is a form of self-judgment, and when we judge ourselves we feel miserable. Here are some common things people say to themselves:

"I'm no good."

"I'm fat and ugly."

"I never do anything right."

"I should never have been born."

"I would be better off dead."

You see how this escalates and causes you to feel miserable. Yet it is so common to think negative thoughts that you can almost say it is normal. In India, they call this the chattering monkey on your shoulder because he won't stop talking. Other people call it their demon or shadow-self. I call it the parasite because it lives within my mind. It is really difficult to get rid of the parasite because he has a willing host. The best thing you can do is to ignore it and carry on with what you are doing. This takes a lot of practice, of course, and it will not happen immediately. But persevere if you want to change your self-talk. And change your life.

Another thing you can journal about is how you are feeling that day. If you want to become aware of your emotions, sit down and close your eyes then feel what is going on in your body. Concentrate. Is your stomach in knots? Do you have a lump in your throat? Do you have a pain in your back? What is your body telling you?

Ask yourself what you are feeling. This is likely to be much harder than you think. Sometimes we are not aware of what we are feeling at all. Are you feeling sad, mad or glad? Name your feelings out loud.

Some families allow feelings of happiness, joy, pleasure and abundance, but do not allow feelings of sadness, anger, or fear in their children's lives. We get so used to this,we suppress certain emotions, and when we grow up, we find it impossible to feel them at all. Write all this down in your journal.

Many emotions have a different meaning so can seem very

difficult to understand. For example, anxiety can come from insecurity, anger can be all about sadness, and shame can be about anger or guilt. If you want to discuss this with your therapist, please do so.

Things like smoking, drinking, taking drugs, eating, and excessive sex may just be a smoke screen hiding your true emotions. People who have an eating addiction, for example, often feel lonely and unaccepted. Or sometimes, if they are overweight, they eat in excess to keep people away, especially people of the opposite sex.

Stop judging your feelings. Accept you have feelings just like everybody else, and it is okay to validate them. Be your own best friend. Curing the habit of feeling bad takes time and compassion. We are not used to feeling empathy with ourselves, but if we can stand back when we are suffering and find some self-compassion, it will go a long way to getting an emotional balance.

Write all these things down in your journal.

Also, learn to sit with your emotions. It may be uncomfortable – you may want to get up and move around, but see if you can sit there and BE in the moment. Some emotions are very difficult to sit with, but they are the ones we need to process the most.

When I was visiting my brother in Australia some years ago, I hated to say goodbye as I knew I wasn't going to see him again – we are both getting old and can't easily travel with health conditions. When I was sitting on the plane I felt an overwhelming sadness come over me. It would have been very easy to ask for a drink, look out of the window, read the in-flight magazine, or even talk to my neighbor, but I decided to sit quietly with the feeling of sadness. It was difficult, I can't lie, all kinds of things went on in my body, but I was able to process my feelings and accept the future.

Another thing you can journal is listening to your quieter emotions. Underneath the major emotions often sits emotions that don't immediately make themselves known. For example, you may be very angry about something and this is causing you to ruminate and think nonstop about your anger. The way to get off the roundabout is to take a deep breath and see if you can understand the quieter emotions that are not easily heard.

Some of the quieter emotions causing anger might be disappointment, regret, shame, or irritability. Write those down in your journal and think about where they came from. When did you last feel those emotions? What was the cause of them? Once you acknowledge these feelings, they may disappear.

Recently, I got annoyed because my cat who was once a very loving lap cat decided not to sit on my lap for a week or so. Instead she would walk all over me, then jump down. This annoyed me no end, and I got fed up with her walking over my legs. Then I sat quietly and thought about why I was so annoyed, and realized that I was sad she didn't want to sit on my lap anymore. It was a bit embarrassing to admit to myself, as sadness is not an emotion we want to feel, but when I was able to sit with this sadness it soon dissipated. I am pleased to report that my cat is back on my lap, and all that annoyance has gone!

These things are great for journaling. You can learn a lot about yourself. Self-knowledge is a fine thing.

It is also a good idea to keep a mood chart, detailing what mood you are in, what medications you take, any physical symptoms you might have, and your bed times, etc. You can find many free versions of mood charts online, or you can chart your symptoms on an app on your phone.

PART THREE

Making Lists

I don't know about you, but I love making lists. I make lists of everything. Of course, I make shopping lists and would never dream of walking into a store without my list! But I also love making lists of birthdays and people I need to send Christmas cards to. I also make lists of things I need to do in the house, and my meal plans for the week.

Anything I can make a list of, I do it. Then, of course, there is always the "to-do" list! That can get too long.

I think it is much easier to read a list than to read a whole book. Then you can put your own take on it to suit yourself. I have provided blank sheets of paper so that you can write your own lists down.

I have made a list of Valuable Tips on getting well and staying well. These are ways you can take control of your life. I am sure you can add to this list.

The Daily Maintenance Plan is concerned with your body and mind, and your way of being in the world. It covers a lot of things you can do each day to make a difference in how you feel.

The Wellness Tool Box list is a great place to put the things that have helped you in the past. And things you might like to try in the future. Think positive thoughts, and be kind to one another is a good start. Give yourself a hug. If you don't know how to do that, I will tell you. Stand or sit still, put your arms around yourself and squeeze. That's probably the best hug you will ever have. Rinse and repeat.

The lists of how you are when you are well and how you are when you are ill are self-explanatory. But when you are depressed, it is great to take out your list of how you are when you are feeling well. It reminds you that you do have good times, and depression can be a thing of the past. You will see that you are a good person and there is still hope for things to get better.

You can make many lists about getting well and staying well, and I have included a few here. These lists are all the things I do to stay well, but you don't have to go by my list, you can either cross my items out, add to these items, or make your own list on the blank sheets of paper in the book. Don't forget to make your own lists. You will be glad you did.

My most important list is the list of my supporters. I keep this list close by just in case I need to get in touch with someone. I may not be in crisis, but I want to know who I can talk to. Talking things over really helps with your mood. Having a nice, friendly chat is great! My list will be different to your list, so you can make your own list of supporters. If you don't have many supporters, think about who you know who would be there for you if you need them. Your best supporter is yourself.

The worst times I had were when I was totally alone with my depression. Loneliness can be very painful, and I have written a book about it called "A Practical Guide to Overcoming Loneliness." I hope you are not lonely, but if you are my book may be of comfort to you. Anyway, when I was alone in my house, I would say to myself, "I don't have anybody to call to tell them I don't have anybody to call." That sure brought tears to my eyes, and I don't recommend it.

Remember, these are my lists so you can cross off what does not apply to you.

Good luck with your lists. You can journal some of the things in the lists every day. Or put the lists on your mirror or on the fridge. Put lists where you can see them.

Don't forget to look at them!

Valuable Tips

- [ ] Use Lists
- [ ] Maintain A Time Management System
- [ ] Set Goals And Priorities
- [ ] Build Strong Relationships With Others
- [ ] Do The Worst Things First
- [ ] Identify Time-Wasters And Eliminate Them
- [ ] Take Control Of Your Emotions
- [ ] Organize Your Home And Office
- [ ] Learn To Say "No."
- [ ] Delegate
- [ ] Use The Right Equipment For The Job
- [ ] Don't Get Distracted – Just Do It
- [ ] Declutter Your House

Notes

Daily Maintenance Plan

- ☐ Go To Bed And Get Up At The Same Time Every Day
- ☐ Stick To A Morning Routine
- ☐ Take Your Medications Daily
- ☐ Put Structure Into Your Day
- ☐ Eat A Good Diet
- ☐ Eat Regular Meals
- ☐ Write In Your Journal
- ☐ Check In – Physically, Emotionally And Mentally
- ☐ Connect With Others
- ☐ Sit In The Sun For 15 Minutes Every Day
- ☐ Drink Plenty Of Water
- ☐ Play Soothing Music
- ☐ Relax
- ☐ Do Regular Exercise
- ☐ Do Something Creative
- ☐ Play With Your Pets

Notes

Wellness Toolbox (Coping Skills)

- ☐ Take Medications At The Same Time Each Day
- ☐ Make Good Financial Decisions (Or Get Help With Finances)
- ☐ Clean One Room Of The House Every Day
- ☐ Keep Doctor's Appointments
- ☐ Connect With A Therapist
- ☐ Pray Or Meditate
- ☐ Educate Yourself About Bipolar
- ☐ Go Out For Coffee Or Lunch With A Friend
- ☐ Do Hobbies
- ☐ Watch Comedies
- ☐ Advocate For Yourself
- ☐ Give Up Smoking And Taking Drugs
- ☐ Have A Positive Attitude
- ☐ Practice Mindfulness

- [ ] Stay In Control Of Your Life
- [ ] Reach Out For Support
- [ ] Volunteer
- [ ] Deep Breathing
- [ ] Journal
- [ ] Keep A Gratitude Journal
- [ ] Be Kind To Yourself And Others
- [ ] Think Positive Thoughts
- [ ] Take A Warm Bath
- [ ] Get And Give A Hug
- [ ] Go For A Walk
- [ ] Work On Your Routine
- [ ] Get Dressed In The House
- [ ] Only Do Three Things In One Day
- [ ] Praise Yourself For Getting Well

Notes

Notes

This Is What I Am Like When I Am Well

- [ ] Happy
- [ ] Confident
- [ ] Cheerful
- [ ] Compassionate
- [ ] Open To New Things
- [ ] Non-Judgemental
- [ ] Content With My Life
- [ ] Understanding Of Others
- [ ] Relaxed
- [ ] Energetic
- [ ] Creative
- [ ] Grounded
- [ ] Social
- [ ] Ambitious
- [ ] Focused
- [ ] Competent
- [ ] Responsible
- [ ] Helpful
- [ ] Calm
- [ ] Positive
- [ ] Grateful
- [ ] Blessed

Notes

This Is What I Am Like When I Am Ill

- ☐ In A Bad Mood
- ☐ Irritable
- ☐ Angry
- ☐ Bad Tempered
- ☐ Rage
- ☐ Depressed
- ☐ Manic
- ☐ Suicidal
- ☐ Discontented
- ☐ Judgemental
- ☐ Bored
- ☐ Nit-Picking
- ☐ Accusatory
- ☐ Lonely
- ☐ Desperate
- ☐ Discontented
- ☐ In Pain
- ☐ Insomnia
- ☐ Overeating
- ☐ Sorry For Myself
- ☐ Suicidal
- ☐ Exhausted

Notes

My Supporters

- My Therapist
- My Psychiatrist
- My Family Doctor
- The Mental Health Clinic
- My Dentist
- People At The Bank
- My Brother Peter
- My Nephew Russell
- My Niece Julie
- Pam
- Cathy
- Kathy
- Marion
- Sean

Notes

PART FOUR

Coping with the Symptoms of Bipolar

This book is designed to help you with all the symptoms of bipolar, so I have divided it up into the following subjects:

Depression
Mania/Hypomania
Psychosis
Anxiety
Panic
Anger/Rage
Pain

And I have further divided it up into the following:

Triggers
Symptoms
Action Plan

The lists are for people with bipolar 1 and bipolar 2. They are not separate. The only difference is that people with bipolar 1 will sometimes have psychosis. People with bipolar 2 don't usually get psychosis, but if they do, they may need another diagnosis. Other than that, the lists are the same for both conditions. You may be lucky and not have anxiety, panic, rage etc. but I have included it here just in case.

These lists are here to help you get well and stay well with bipolar. It is up to you how much you use these lists. You must remember, like in part 3, these are my lists and you may not have everything on the list. This is okay. Just add to my list or make your own list as before. I have provided blank sheets for this purpose.

When you have gone through this whole book, you will have a better chance of getting well and staying well with bipolar.

Depression

If you have bipolar, you will no doubt have depression as bipolar has two moods – depression and mania/hypomania. The exception to this rule is the rare person who has bipolar 1 with no depression at all. Other than that, people with bipolar will suffer a number of episodes of depression in their lifetime.

People with major depressive disorder (clinical depression) do not have mania/hypomania as it is a unipolar illness with only one mood. It is said that these people have more chronic forms of depression, but I don't know of any research that is being done on this at present. Either way, depression is terrible for the sufferer, and for the people in their lives.

You may be one of the lucky ones who has a group of supporters. These people are always there for you, no matter what sort of mood you are in. But it is difficult for them to know how to react when you are depressed if they have never walked in your shoes. It is easy to say the wrong thing and make the situation worse, especially when the depression is severe. They may cause you to feel even more guilty than you do already because you cannot get well to order. There is no magic wand to cure bipolar. If someone is insisting you get well, you can say, "Believe me, I would get well if I could. Depression is not easy to live with."

Many people don't know what to say when their loved one is depressed. If you find the people around you have no understanding of your illness, do print out some information for them, or let them read this book.

If you are so ill you cannot get out of bed, even the most patient person has no idea how to handle that situation. By that time, I hope you will have seen your doctor and he/she has started you on medication and you are getting therapy. If you are severely depressed, you may have to be admitted to a hospital to keep you safe and to change your medication.

I would suggest you read up on bipolar when you are well and make sure you understand that your moods are not your fault. It is part of the illness.

You may be unlucky, and not have any support at all. That is very hard to live with. I was one of those people for many years as even though I told people about my illness they were not prepared to help me when I got sick. However, I finally found a therapist who helped me get through my depressive episodes. He was very helpful indeed.

I also found many members of my family on Facebook, and it has been a revelation. I have never been happier in my life as I felt very alone before. They were not there to help with the moods I used to get, though, as they do not understand bipolar, but it is good to know I am cared about now.

When do your depressions start? Are they brought on by a life event, or are they spontaneous and appear with no apparent reason? You may have both forms of depression. This illness can be a response to challenging situations in your life, or it can come out of nowhere.

What things can bring on a depression? Well, that could be one of many things. You may have lost a loved one, or your job, or got a divorce, or your child may have stopped talking to you and you are estranged. These are major life events. You can understand, to some degree, that these are situations that would make anybody depressed. But the thing about bipolar depression is it is far more severe than the ordinary person's "bad day." And it can go on for a very long time, with no end in sight.

Then there are the life situations that are not quite as serious, but nevertheless bring on a depressive episode. There are things like the weather – many people's depressions are influenced by the weather, especially in the winter months – or you may have had to miss a wedding because you didn't feel well, or you may have had a nasty bout of the flu, or any number of other things that are all part of life, but can have a major effect on you when you have bipolar.

It is also true that with bipolar you can have depressions that come on out of nowhere, even when things are going well. This can cause a great deal of guilt because you think you should feel happy when you are not. These depressive episodes can creep up on you without warning, or they can occur immediately after a manic/hypomanic episode which is often the case.

As bipolar is a cyclical disease, depression may well be spontaneous. You may be "lucky" in that you only get depressed once a year, but many other people get depressed every few months or weeks, and some other people get depressed every day, sometimes once an hour. There is no telling how bipolar will affect you. I hope this book will help you cope, and possibly lengthen the time between episodes.

I noticed the first thing to affect me when I became depressed was that I would get very clumsy and start bumping into things and dropping things. I don't know if this is common, but it always heralded my depressions. Also, my writing changed, and I found that I was writing a tiny scrawl like an ant had crawled over the page.

After that it was lack of energy. It hit me like a ton of bricks. I suddenly couldn't walk across the room without great difficulty. I am sure this has happened to you at one time or another as lack of energy is very common in depression. It is a disturbing symptom because it can interfere with your normal daily life. If you start to feel this lethargy when you have to go to work or look after children in the home, it is very difficult to cope with. Your legs feel like lead and you can hardly keep your head up at all.

This is not a symptom the average person can understand. Why would you get so tired? What is causing this tiredness? Yet, no matter how hard you try, you are devoid of energy and have a hard time coping with every day life. People at school or in college have a hard time with this symptom as all they want to do is go back to bed.

Be diligent and go to bed early so that you can get a good night's sleep.

The next thing I notice is my bad temper. I am usually a calm person and not easily ruffled, but when I used to get depressed, I became very irritable indeed. Every little thing set me off, and this may well happen to you. This is very bad if you have to go to work because you can't be irritable with everybody around you, or you will soon get your marching orders. Yet this irritability will not leave you alone.

Challenging emotions accompany depression. Everybody gets them. You feel guilty, angry, hopeless, helpless and worthless. These feelings are so prevalent, you don't think you will ever get through them. But if you can hang onto a modicum of truth, you will know you were able to get through your previous depression, and you will do so again. The worst thing with bipolar is to give up hope. There is always hope for a brighter day tomorrow. Take it one day at a time.

Lack of motivation is hard to live with as well. You have no interest in things that used to interest you. Nothing appeals to you. People will tell you to go out and meet people, but you do not want to meet people when you are depressed. And you are very likely to isolate so meeting people is out of the question. You are likely to lose your interest in eating as well. Nothing appeals to you, or you just eat for the sake of eating. This can be a dangerous sign of deep depression and can badly affect your health. If you lose 5 - 10% of your body weight you can be very ill indeed, and will need to see your doctor. The reverse is also true. Some people can't stop eating when depressed and gain a lot of weight. You will need to discuss this with your doctor.

One thing that is very disturbing are thought of death and suicide. You may think you are the only one who is feeling this way, but feeling suicidal is just another symptom of bipolar and should be treated as such. But with every symptom comes an action, and suicidal thoughts are no different. Before you do anything to yourself do call someone. If you have a friend to call, or a professional person, call them and tell them how you feel. If this is not possible call the Suicide Prevention and Crisis Lifeline on 988. At one time, they had a long number that nobody could remember, but 988 is easy to remember when you feel ill.

If you feel suicidal do take precautions and put all dangerous things out of your reach. No medication, guns, knives or anything that could harm you should be left unattended in the house. If you are not able to do this for yourself, be sure to get someone else to do it for you. Also, try to get someone to stay with you when you feel suicidal as mistakes can be made, and lives can be lost unintentionally.

Please remember that suicidal ideation is just another part of bipolar. But you need to act on getting rid of it fast.

If you feel a bout of depression coming on, do get in touch with your doctor or psychiatrist and start a treatment plan. The sooner you start taking medication the better as it can take two to four weeks to work.

Here follows my lists for **Triggers**, **Symptoms** and **Action Plans** for all the symptoms of bipolar, not just depression. Remember these are my lists, but you can change the ones that don't apply to you, or write on the blank sheets of paper.

Suicide Prevention and Crisis Lifeline – 988

Triggers

- [ ] Mess
- [ ] Chaos
- [ ] Losing things
- [ ] Dropping things
- [ ] Financial problems
- [ ] Thinking about the future
- [ ] Clutter
- [ ] Criticism
- [ ] Pain
- [ ] Feeling invisible
- [ ] Old age
- [ ] Feeling left out
- [ ] Put downs
- [ ] Rejection
- [ ] Being judged
- [ ] Crowds
- [ ] Too much to do
- [ ] Overwhelmed
- [ ] Paperwork
- [ ] Feeling alone
- [ ] Filling in forms
- [ ] Coming out of the hospital
- [ ] Isolating
- [ ] Ruminating

Notes

Symptoms

- [ ] Quit cooking meals
- [ ] Wanting chocolate
- [ ] Can't sleep or sleep too much
- [ ] Don't want to do anything
- [ ] Sad, guilty and worthleass
- [ ] Fighting with people
- [ ] No motivation
- [ ] Confusion
- [ ] Suicidal thoughts
- [ ] Easily startled
- [ ] Feeling very lonely
- [ ] No appetite
- [ ] Shaking
- [ ] Worried about money
- [ ] Can't get my breath
- [ ] Not washing my hair
- [ ] Feel like a failure
- [ ] Don't tidy up
- [ ] People annoy me
- [ ] Exhaustion
- [ ] Clumsy
- [ ] Irritable
- [ ] Can't stop crying
- [ ] Isolating
- [ ] Can't think clearly
- [ ] Obsessed with negative thoughts
- [ ] Can't concentrate
- [ ] Feeling needy
- [ ] Pain in my back
- [ ] Ruminating about the past
- [ ] Feel as if I am drowning
- [ ] Fear of the future
- [ ] Not showering
- [ ] Can't walk straight

Notes

Action Plan

- [ ] Watch You Tube videos
- [ ] Do some crafts
- [ ] Do some sewing
- [ ] Do some flower arranging
- [ ] Listen to podcasts
- [ ] Sleep
- [ ] Take a walk
- [ ] Do some jig-saw puzzles
- [ ] Call friends
- [ ] Look through photo albums
- [ ] Do some creative visualization
- [ ] Do only 3 things in one day
- [ ] Rest
- [ ] Make piles of paperwork to do later
- [ ] Make a list
- [ ] Laugh at myself
- [ ] Breathe
- [ ] Call the crisis line
- [ ] Take a bubble bath
- [ ] Do some painting
- [ ] Get a pedicure
- [ ] Get a massage
- [ ] Do some coloring books
- [ ] Do some exercise
- [ ] Sit in the sun
- [ ] Do online Solitaire
- [ ] Write to online friends
- [ ] Do some relaxation exercises
- [ ] Light candles
- [ ] Go with the flow
- [ ] Play relaxing music
- [ ] Take a nap
- [ ] Journal
- [ ] Smile
- [ ] Accept everything in my life
- [ ] Ask for help
- [ ] Watch Netflix

Notes

Mania/Hypomania

People with bipolar 1 get true mania, whereas people with bipolar 2 get hypomania. The difference is not immediately understood as the two are so similar. Mania and hypomania have the same symptoms, but people with hypomania are better able to function in their every day lives than people with bipolar 1. Mania can get out of control very quickly.

People with bipolar 2 hypomanias can often be very productive and creative, whereas people with mania can start a lot of projects at once but never finish them. When I had mania, I used to always start reading at least six books at once. I couldn't concentrate on one book, but couldn't finish the other books either. I had piles of books with book marks in them laying around the house. This may well apply to you.

This also applied to do-it-yourself projects. I was very keen to do things in my house when I was manic. At one time, I painted all my kitchen cabinets on my own. I started them in mania, but ran out of steam half way through and had to finish them when I was depressed. I couldn't leave cabinets with no doors on, could I?

It is usually easier to hold down a job if you have bipolar 2 hypomania, but very difficult in mania. Of course, there are always exceptions to the rule – I myself was able to carry out the duties of an RN for eleven years with bipolar 1. I can't remember any manic episodes as at the time I was fairly well. Some people with mania can hold down a job quite well. If you think of all the entertainers with bipolar on my list below, you will see that these people did not get a month off for manic episodes:

Kanye West, Mariah Carey, Carrie Fisher, Mel Gibson, Demi Lovato, Maria Bamford, Catherine Zeta-Jones, Frank Sinatra, David LaChapelle, Sinead O'Connor, Jean-Claude Van Damme, Jane Pauley, Patty Duke, Linda Hamilton, Mariette Hartley, Selena Gomez, Scott Stapp, Maurice Benard, David Harbour, Amy Winehouse, Halsey, Richard Dreyfuss, Russell Brand, Kurt Cobain, Grahame Greene, Nina Simone, Sir. Winston Churchill, Vincent Van Gogh, Virginia Wolf, Ernest Hemingway, Buzz Aldrin, Florence Nightingale, Sting, Isaac Newton, William Blake, Beethoven, Theodore Roosevelt

People in a hypomanic episode can be very productive indeed. They may be very talkative and have ideas flowing all the time, but they can also achieve many important and creative tasks like writing books or painting accomplished works of art. As the hypomania doesn't accelerate into mania, they can get a lot done.

Also, at work they can apply themselves and excel very easily. This is when people get a raise! But, of course, if the hypomania escalates, the job will likely be lost. It is not uncommon for people with bipolar to have 10 jobs over a short period of time, and to only be able to last in one position from four to six months. I remember those times very well as it was difficult to work with mania.

To me the worst thing about mania is that everything is sped up. Thoughts and ideas come thick and fast, and the pressure to talk all the time is apparent. Many people with mania are unable to stop interrupting people, or their speech gets so fast it becomes unintelligible. This obviously brings a startled reaction from the people close to you, or your colleagues at work. Who can keep up with a person with bipolar mania?

I always found that other people appeared to be talking and walking very slowly indeed. In fact everything they were doing looked ridiculously slow. I used to become very impatient with them and try to speed them up which didn't go down well at all.

The mood can be elevated or irritable in mania. When the mood is elevated you can feel on top of the world, and think you are somebody special like the King, or even God. Many people become very religious, or even clairvoyant during periods of mania, and they try to push these things onto other people.

Mania can make you feel exuberant and omnipotent. It is a wonderful feeling like floating on a cloud. I remember telling somebody I was having the best day of my life for no apparent reason except that I felt as if I was floating on a cloud.

You may also became hypersexual when manic, and this is very common. Somehow the lack of sexual energy in depression is replaced by heightened sexual interest in mania. Everybody looks as if they are entranced by you, and you flirt with people you don't know. Some of this behavior can be harmless, but people also sleep with people they don't know which can put a real strain on any relationship. And the addition of STDs or an unwanted child can break up a marriage altogether. Yet there is nothing you can do if you are feeling like this, except to stay at home and wait for the mania to pass! Sometimes medication works, but I think sexual energy is very powerful indeed.

If you have been hypersexual in mania and thought you were the exception to the rule, be comforted to know that you are certainly not the only one who has felt like that. Whether you act on it or not can be the difference between a rewarding partnership or one that breaks down.

This applies to risk-taking as well. This symptom is very difficult to control with mania. Some people spend their life savings to take trips around the world. They do not plan these trips, or tell their partner where they are going. All that is left when they return is a broken relationship and an empty bank account.

Gambling is common as well, and so are bad business deals. Both can put you in the red in the bank.

Road rage and shopping to excess are also features of mania. I have suffered with both of these things and so have many other people. I don't need to tell you the risks involved in road rage, and the consequences of buying things you don't need. This is where it is helpful to put things in your cart on Amazon when you are manic, then you can decide whether to buy them or not when the mania passes. But to have that much control is rare. I used to leave my credit cards with the bank when I felt mania coming on and they were happy to hold on to them for me.

Once I traded in my perfectly nice car that was already paid for, and bought two cars on loans in one week. That is a bit excessive, I am sure you will agree.

Another thing that is almost certainly likely to suffer is sleep. When you have mania, there is no interest in sleep. In fact, you think if you sleep, you will be missing out on something important. Having three or four hours sleep, and waking up refreshed is very common in bipolar mania. If you start to lose sleep for a couple of days in a row, it is likely you are about to have a manic episode. This is the time to call the doctor and change your medication.

The energy in mania is the exact opposite from that in depression, and it is not unusual to find a manic person scrubbing the grout in between the floor tiles at three in the morning. Sorting out cupboards and drawers is a popular past time in mania as well.

All this sounds like fun, but it can get out of hand very quickly and you can find yourself in the hospital having your medication changed. The problem is you do not feel ill when manic. How can you be ill when you feel so wonderful? But you are ill, and it can get out of control very quickly.

When bipolar mania is severe, you can begin to have psychosis which is quite common in bipolar 1. It can also be found in a severe depression, even in major depressive disorder.

Psychosis is a frightening experience as you lose touch with reality. The way you see the world is totally different from the way others experience it. This is because hallucinations accompany psychosis. If you have ever had hallucinations you will know how terrible this is. There is no way to describe them to a person who has never experienced it because it is not possible to explain it. The senses become distorted and you quite possibly begin to smell strange things. Along with this you can hear your name being called but there is nobody there. You can taste and touch things that are not real, along with seeing things materialize before you.

I have had many experiences with psychosis and have been in the hospital again and again to stop it. If you have bipolar 1, it is likely that you have experienced psychosis as well. One strange thing is I was able to hold down a job as a publicity assistant with psychosis! I can't imagine how I did it now.

As I said in the beginning, mania is not always a positive experience. Many people experience irritability, anger and rage when manic. This feeling of being out of control is very hard to bear. It seems as if you can never get the anger under control, and the rage is terrible. There are medications to help with this, though, so it is best to call the doctor to change your medicines when you feel this coming on.

I have also been told that anxiety can precipitate mania, but I have no experience of that. You may have had that yourself and I would be pleased to hear of it. Again your best resource is your doctor who will be able to provide you with medication to control the anxiety.

Triggers

- ☐ Looking at items on Amazon
- ☐ Driving too fast
- ☐ Buying DIY stuff at Home Depot
- ☐ Buying stuff at Dollar Tree
- ☐ Starting to read six books at once
- ☐ Starting new projects
- ☐ Not tired
- ☐ Feeling extremely happy
- ☐ Ideas coming quickly
- ☐ Hungry all the time
- ☐ Fits of anger
- ☐ Benevolent feelings towards others
- ☐ Going shopping
- ☐ Buying art supplies
- ☐ Buying furniture
- ☐ Walking into car showrooms
- ☐ Can't concentrate
- ☐ No time to eat proper meals
- ☐ Talking very fast
- ☐ Feel irritated
- ☐ Getting bored easily
- ☐ Flirting with the opposite sex
- ☐ Doing large, loopy hand writing

Notes

Symptoms

- [ ] Can't sleep
- [ ] Ordering things online
- [ ] Talking and thinking fast
- [ ] Starting new projects
- [ ] Doing major cleaning
- [ ] Mess/chaos everywhere
- [ ] Impulsive
- [ ] Phoning a lot of people
- [ ] Driving badly
- [ ] Can't concentrate
- [ ] Racing round the house out of breath
- [ ] Spending money
- [ ] Angry outbursts
- [ ] People seem slow and stupid
- [ ] Doing sorting projects
- [ ] Thoughts of self-harm
- [ ] Driving too fast
- [ ] Writing lots of emails
- [ ] Risk-taking
- [ ] Being irrational
- [ ] Agitated, can't relax
- [ ] Flirting

Notes

Action Plan

- [ ] Become aware
- [ ] Say a mantra - slow down
- [ ] Check out plans with another
- [ ] Relax
- [ ] Take some days off work
- [ ] Do some meditation
- [ ] Believe people who say you are ill
- [ ] Don't drive unnecessarily
- [ ] STOP
- [ ] Put credit cards in safe place
- [ ] Stop and take deep breaths
- [ ] Do some exercise
- [ ] Lie down and take a nap
- [ ] Do creative visualization
- [ ] See your doctor

Notes

Mixed Features (mixed episode)

Most people have two bipolar moods: depression and mania, but about a third to a half experience what is now called bipolar with mixed features. This is experiencing both depression and mania at the same time, or in quick succession. You can go from euphoria to despair in a matter of minutes. This is like being on a roller coaster, and can be very distressing.

You may find you cannot relax and feel agitated, at the same time as feeling sad and hopeless. These are symptoms of both mania and depression. Symptoms of psychosis can also appear at the same time which makes treatment very difficult. If you have a mixed episode, you will need to see your doctor immediately in order to catch it before it takes hold.

Your doctor will have to treat both mania and depression at the same time, so there is room for error. But it is imperative that you start treatment early to avoid hospitalization.

It would also be wise to see a therapist to help you cope with life on a daily basis.

Mixed episodes can be very dangerous and hard to treat, so get help quickly. Suicidal thoughts are more common in mixed episodes.

Triggers

- [ ] Insomnia
- [ ] Doing too much
- [ ] Obsessions
- [ ] Compulsive
- [ ] Suddenly feeling very creative
- [ ] Multi-tasking
- [ ] Exhaustion
- [ ] Frenetic energy/tired at the same time
- [ ] Doing lots of paperwork
- [ ] Starting lots of projects, can't follow throughout

Notes

Symptoms

- [ ] Can't sleep
- [ ] Angry
- [ ] High energy
- [ ] Racing speech
- [ ] Irrational
- [ ] Wanting to spend a lot of money
- [ ] Poor decision-making
- [ ] Feel like you must climb out of your skin
- [ ] Eyes flickering
- [ ] Feeling of doom
- [ ] Extreme worry about money
- [ ] Organizing clutter
- [ ] Scared of the future
- [ ] Suicidal
- [ ] Making suicide plans
- [ ] Extreme agitation
- [ ] Nervousness
- [ ] Racing thoughts
- [ ] Irritated
- [ ] Racing through a to-do list
- [ ] Can't relax
- [ ] Desperate for help
- [ ] Wanting to be somewhere else
- [ ] Can't catch my breath
- [ ] Chewing my lips
- [ ] Loads of ideas for projects
- [ ] Panic state
- [ ] Sad
- [ ] Can't think clearly
- [ ] Crying

Notes

Action Plan

- [ ] STOP
- [ ] Wash your face in cold water
- [ ] Drink water
- [ ] Read ONE book at a time
- [ ] Journal
- [ ] Observe your emotions
- [ ] Play relaxation tapes
- [ ] Creative visualization
- [ ] Watch comedies
- [ ] Use stress balls
- [ ] Deep breathing exercises
- [ ] Do muscle relaxation exercises
- [ ] Stay at home
- [ ] Don't worry about mess

Notes

Psychosis

We have touched on this before, and I have described what it is like to have psychosis. Simply put, psychosis is a break in reality – not knowing what is real and what is not.

Psychosis occurs mostly in bipolar 1, affecting 50% to 75% of people. But people with bipolar 2 can also experience it when they are severely depressed. The same applies to people with major depressive disorder.

People with bipolar 1 can develop psychosis along with a severe episode of mania or depression. It is difficult to tell when the mania or depression has progressed to psychosis. And is not usually perceived by the patient as everything seems normal on the surface. If you are having symptoms, they seem real to you.

Psychosis is one of the main symptoms experienced by people with schizophrenia, but people with bipolar 1 only have psychosis on a temporary basis with a severe manic or depressive episode. Nevertheless, it should be treated as soon as possible as it can take a couple of weeks for treatment to work.

If you have psychosis you will likely be experiencing hallucinations, delusions and/or paranoia.

Hallucinations affect the senses, and it is not unusual to see strange shapes and objects. It also affects your hearing, your sense of smell, taste and touch. You might hear your name being called when there's no-one there, or hear a choir singing inside your head. You might also feel bugs creeping over or inside your skin and have a taste like metal or blood in your mouth. These experiences can be very alarming.

With delusions, you will believe things that are not true, but no amount of reasoning can change your perception. Logic does not work in psychosis. Nothing is logical. It is like living in a different universe. However, some people are able to carry on with their life as if nothing strange is happening.

Paranoia can take many forms, but it generally means people are out to get the person. They can believe that the walls are bugged, people can hear what they are thinking, or the CIA is following them.

People with psychosis feel very alone and confused about their experiences because no matter what other people tell them, everything seems real.

Every day living become difficult because what everybody else takes for granted, like sleeping, eating and keeping up with good hygiene, does not seem important to you anymore. Sleep is often hard to come by, there may well be a loss of interest in food (often due to a strange taste in the mouth,) and hygiene no longer interests you. It can be difficult to approach the person with these difficulties because they no longer see these things as important.

Psychosis can be mood congruent or mood in-congruent. Mood congruent is psychosis affected by your present mood, be it depression or mania. If you are in a manic mood, for example, you might experience feelings of grandeur, or think you are Jesus Christ or Princess Diana. In a depressive mood, you might feel very guilty.

But in-congruent psychosis doesn't match your mood. You might be depressed, but laugh when your dog dies. Or you may be depressed but hear someone telling you that you are someone special chosen by God.

Mood in-congruent psychosis is more dangerous and more difficult to treat. And the incidence of suicide is more likely. This is the most dangerous form of the illness, and the person should be carefully monitored.

Mood stabilizers and anti-psychotics are often the best treatment, but if the psychosis doesn't clear up, you might need to go to the hospital where ECT (electroconvulsive therapy), among other treatments, can be tried.

It is also a good idea to have some family or talk therapy to discover what is or is not real.

I went to the hospital quite a few times with in-congruent psychosis where I was depressed, but couldn't stop talking and cracking jokes.

If you are prone to psychosis, make out a list of your symptoms for your supporters so that they can call the doctor for you.

Triggers (prodromal phase of psychosis before the person gets sick.)

- [ ] Difficulty screening out information and sensations
- [ ] Suddenly unattached to anybody or anything
- [ ] Strange things going on around you
- [ ] Not understanding what is being said
- [ ] People seem far away
- [ ] Totally lost interest in everything
- [ ] Depressed mood
- [ ] Feeling overwhelmed
- [ ] Unexplained difficulties at work or school
- [ ] Desire to be alone
- [ ] Nothing seems real
- [ ] Don't need anybody
- [ ] Not recognizing people
- [ ] Can't concentrate to read
- [ ] Don't feel the need to contact anyone
- [ ] Feeling disconnected
- [ ] Irritability
- [ ] Sleep disturbances
- [ ] Suspiciousness
- [ ] Unable to understand others

Notes

Symptoms

- [ ] Obsessions
- [ ] Seeing things that aren't there
- [ ] Finding coincidences everywhere
- [ ] Smelling burning
- [ ] Hearing things that are not there
- [ ] Deluded people are talking about you
- [ ] Things disappear, then reappear
- [ ] Unable to pay bills
- [ ] Irrational responses to others – crying, shouting
- [ ] Saying crazy things
- [ ] Think things have been moved
- [ ] Think people have stolen from you
- [ ] Feeling spaced out
- [ ] Not trusting of anybody
- [ ] Not trusting the system – police, hospital
- [ ] Hearing voices or singing

Notes

Action Plan

- [ ] STOP!
- [ ] Check irrational thoughts
- [ ] Talk to somebody
- [ ] Rest
- [ ] Do your Daily Management Plan
- [ ] Make a list of things you can do to help yourself
- [ ] Suicide Prevention and Crisis Lifeline - 988
- [ ] See your doctor
- [ ] Call 911

Notes

Psychosis

– Dissociation/Early Warning Signs

- ☐ Strange feelings as if you are in a dream or play
- ☐ Nothing seems real
- ☐ Total loss of interest in anything
- ☐ Suddenly totally unattached to anybody or anything
- ☐ Don't feel the need to contact people
- ☐ Don't need anybody
- ☐ People seem far away
- ☐ Strange feelings in the body
- ☐ Can't concentrate
- ☐ Strange things going on around you
- ☐ Not understanding what is said
- ☐ Not recognizing people

See a doctor as soon as possible.

Notes

Anxiety

There are many co-morbid illnesses associated with bipolar, and anxiety is one of them. Anxiety affects about 50% of people with bipolar. It is a very difficult disorder to cope with. Anxiety can take the form of GAD (generalized anxiety disorder), OCD (obsessive, compulsive disorder,) PTSD (Post-traumatic stress disorder) and others. It is hard enough to have to deal with bipolar without the added stress of an anxiety disorder. It can also make bipolar worse and more difficult to treat. Because of this, it is important that the doctor screen the person with both disorders at each visit.

If you have anxiety, you will know it is no use trying to explain it to someone who has never had it. Anxiety affects everything you do.

The symptoms of anxiety are very like mania/hypomania so it can be difficult for the doctor to tell these two illnesses apart. You know the difference, so you must try to tell the doctor which symptoms belong to bipolar and which symptoms belong to anxiety. It is important as the treatment is different. I would try therapy first before taking medications. But should you need to take medications, don't be afraid of them. They can really help you.

Living with anxiety is terrible because it affects everything you do, or in some cases it is so bad that you are shaking even if you are not doing anything. Some people are shaking in their own house even when there is no personal threat.

Anxiety is really about fear, usually fear of the future. I call it the "What if? Disease." What if I can't do a presentation at work? What if I can't speak up at a meeting? What if I can't talk to other parents at my child's school? What if I can't travel away from home? All these things take a certain amount of confidence and that is lost if fear takes over. Anxiety is exhausting and make life miserable.

Triggers

- [ ] Finances
- [ ] Thinking too far in the future
- [ ] Pain
- [ ] Can't get hold of anyone
- [ ] Can't decide what to do next
- [ ] Noise
- [ ] Movement/noise around me
- [ ] Speaking on the phone
- [ ] Can't think clearly
- [ ] Electronics break down
- [ ] Things breaking down
- [ ] Physical problems
- [ ] Loneliness
- [ ] Confusion about taking medications
- [ ] Bright lights
- [ ] Crowds
- [ ] Trying to fill in forms
- [ ] Signing your name
- [ ] Feeling rushed

Notes

Symptoms

- ☐ Shaking
- ☐ Cold and chills
- ☐ Thoughts spinning out of control
- ☐ Fear of other people
- ☐ Sudden loss of confidence
- ☐ Can't make a decision
- ☐ Sense of urgency but don't know what to do
- ☐ Confusion
- ☐ Can't breathe
- ☐ Everything telling me I should act now
- ☐ Feelings of drowning
- ☐ Going into panic mode
- ☐ Dizzy
- ☐ Sweating profusely
- ☐ Can't think straight
- ☐ Can't speak out loud in a crowd
- ☐ Feeling stupid
- ☐ Feelings of your heart being in your mouth
- ☐ Quaking
- ☐ Sinking feeling
- ☐ Things spinning out of control
- ☐ Speeded up
- ☐ Everything seems out of control

Notes

Action Plan

- [ ] Take anxiety medication
- [ ] STOP
- [ ] Do nothing
- [ ] Grounding – Smells
- [ ] Grounding – Sounds
- [ ] Grounding – Feel
- [ ] CATCH IT
- [ ] CHECK IT
- [ ] CHANGE IT
- [ ] Try to focus on something
- [ ] Sit down and breathe
- [ ] Limit stimuli
- [ ] Ask for help
- [ ] Count down from 100
- [ ] Visualize a favorite place
- [ ] Listen to music
- [ ] Wash your face with cold water
- [ ] Focus on your senses
- [ ] Write down your feelings
- [ ] Make a list of problems

Make a list of what you could do to solve your problems.

Check in: How am I:

- Mentally
- Physically
- Emotionally

Notes

Panic Attacks

Panic attacks often stem from anxiety when it gets out of control. However, there is a line of thought these days that panic attacks show themselves before the actual symptoms begin so they are not quite out of the blue. The symptoms you may feel before the start of panic are a sensation of being far away, unable to focus your eyesight, dizzy and spaced out. You may also find yourself with the sensation of looking down on your body.

Panic attacks are different from an anxiety attack. Anxiety attacks stem from excessive anxiety over a period of time until it reaches a crescendo. Whereas panic attacks appear to come out of nowhere (unless you are astute and can spot the symptoms before the attack begins.)

Some people are unlucky and have several panic attacks a day. This is called panic illness or disorder and needs careful monitoring and treatment by a doctor.

Panic attacks are one of the worst experiences you can have in as there is a terrible feeling of being out of control, and a fear of going mad or even dying. This feeling is so strong that it makes the panic attack even worse.

Many hospital visits have arisen out of panic attacks. The person thinks they are having a heart attack as panic attacks have almost the same symptoms. It is wise to go to the hospital, even though you are not having a heart attack. It is better to be safe than sorry.

If you have panic attacks, do see your doctor to get treatment. There is no need to suffer in silence.

Triggers

- [ ] Financial dealings of any kind
- [ ] Feeling abandoned
- [ ] Being late
- [ ] Chaos
- [ ] Loud noises
- [ ] Physical illnesses
- [ ] Visits from certain people
- [ ] Filling in forms
- [ ] Signing your name
- [ ] Losing things
- [ ] Things breaking down
- [ ] Fears of the future
- [ ] Crowds
- [ ] Bright lights
- [ ] Getting medications mixed up
- [ ] Going out with certain people
- [ ] Scams

Notes

Symptoms

- [ ] Can't breathe
- [ ] Shaky
- [ ] Can't think clearly
- [ ] Sweating hands
- [ ] Suddenly lights, noise and crows unbearable
- [ ] Feeling that you are dying
- [ ] Hyperventilating
- [ ] Desperate
- [ ] Cold
- [ ] Dizzy
- [ ] Heart pounding
- [ ] Want to run
- [ ] Feeling like you are going mad
- [ ] A need to feel contained
- [ ] Tearful

Notes

Action Plan

- [ ] Breathe
- [ ] Get out of the situation
- [ ] Close down the computer
- [ ] Smell what is in the environment
- [ ] Take medication given by doctor
- [ ] Go outside – take five minutes before returning
- [ ] Put the phone off of the hook
- [ ] Look at something with intention
- [ ] Listen and distinguish sounds
- [ ] Rest

Notes

Anger and Rage

Anger is a basic human emotion. Like joy, sadness and excitement, we have all felt anger at some time or another. You can plainly see it in little children! I have also noticed that many people have problems with expressing anger in a healthy way, usually because that emotion, along with fear, sadness and frustration, were not tolerated in the family. My family did not tolerate anger at all, so I hid it very successfully for years. Then it bubbled up when my husband died and would not go away.

Anger is part of the fight or flight cycle that is caused by a rush of adrenaline in the body. It is a survival instinct. If a person gets very angry, they will become argumentative or even violent. Others should get themselves out of the situation as this is probably the wisest course of action.

People get angry for other reasons as well: social injustice, entitlement, driving, and low tolerance of discomfort. Anger is also a part of grieving. When a loved one dies, many people become angry with the doctors or nurses who took care of the patient, or themselves, and even the God of their understanding. It may take a while to subside after a death, especially a sudden death where there is no warning that the person will pass.

A lack of sleep can also cause anger, so it is best to pay attention to your sleep pattern if you are an angry person. Deep breathing and counting to ten are helpful, but not often easy to do in a bout of anger.

If the anger gets extreme go on an anger management course.

It is debatable if there is such a thing as bipolar anger or rage, but I tend to think both of these problems are very common in people with bipolar. I did put this to a psychiatrist nurse practitioner once who discounted it, but she did give me a new medication to help it subside. I can't remember which medication, but that doesn't matter, what does matter is that it worked.

I had terrible problems with anger and rage myself. In fact, I was angry the whole time for five years after my husband killed himself. In the end, I had to give it up to the universe. And rage bothered me a lot as well. If you have rage attacks, you will not need me to tell you how frightening they are to yourself and those around you.

Anger can come up out of the blue (acute anger), or can hang around for a long time (chronic). No matter what, it is physically exhausting. It is also emotionally draining. Many people have angry episodes that terrify their partners or their children. Of course, if you are angry at work, you won't last long!

Unfortunately, I cannot cover the whole subject of anger here as it is too much for a book like this. If you have anger it may be sensible to study it. There are heaps of books and articles on the internet about anger.

Triggers

- [ ] Financial problems
- [ ] Being late
- [ ] Losing things
- [ ] Being lectured to
- [ ] Too much to do
- [ ] Appliances not working
- [ ] Being used
- [ ] Being over-tired
- [ ] Not getting your own way
- [ ] Pain
- [ ] Mixed episodes in bipolar disorder
- [ ] Making stupid mistakes
- [ ] Technology
- [ ] Being rushed
- [ ] Told how to run your life
- [ ] Robo calls
- [ ] Politics
- [ ] Crowds
- [ ] Things breaking down
- [ ] Restless leg syndrome
- [ ] Confrontations
- [ ] Chronic pain

Notes

Symptoms

- [ ] Punishing yourself
- [ ] Criticizing yourself
- [ ] Feeling like throwing up
- [ ] Making irrational decisions
- [ ] Feeling hot or cold all over
- [ ] Chewing your lips
- [ ] Chastising yourself
- [ ] Shaking
- [ ] Shouting
- [ ] Can't breathe
- [ ] Gritting your teeth
- [ ] Doing too much

Notes

Action Plan

- ☐ STOP
- ☐ Turn your cell phone off
- ☐ Breathe
- ☐ Make piles of paperwork and put off sorting them
- ☐ Avoid situations that make you angry
- ☐ Visualize your favorite place
- ☐ Wash your face with cold water
- ☐ Read a light-hearted book
- ☐ Focus on your senses
- ☐ Exercise to relax and stretch muscles
- ☐ Think of something that makes you happy
- ☐ Walk away
- ☐ Play relaxing music
- ☐ Drink ice water
- ☐ Say mantras
- ☐ Take a walk
- ☐ Count from 100 down
- ☐ Watch comedies
- ☐ Use a stress ball
- ☐ Distract yourself
- ☐ Name your emotions

Notes

Pain

Pain is not a direct symptom of bipolar disorder, but I have included it here because pain can be felt anywhere in the body when a person is depressed. In fact, bodily aches and pains are very common in bipolar. Many people don't realize that.

Constant pain can make anybody feel angry because there is no obvious way to stop it. You are totally out of control. Constant pain is very wearing on the body and the emotions. Many illnesses have a lot of pain attached to them – cancer, amputation and backaches come to mind. Sometimes, there is nothing that can be done to relieve the pain. No matter what the doctor gives you, it only takes the edge off of it. The very worst pain in the body is said to be trigeminal neuralgia. This is pain of the facial nerve in the lower jaw, and sometimes the nose and eye.

Pain can make you feel very vulnerable. If you have continuous pain no matter what you do for it, you can get to the point where you just want to scream. But of course, that doesn't work. Pain relievers can help, so ask your doctor to prescribe them. In hospice, strong pain killers are given to terminal patients to make them comfortable.

Chronic stress can cause pain because the body becomes overloaded with stress hormones which change the neurochemicals in the brain.

Triggers

- ☐ Doing too much
- ☐ Walking
- ☐ Housework
- ☐ Gardening
- ☐ Stress
- ☐ Certain foods
- ☐ Activities around the house
- ☐ Smoking (direct cause of back pain)
- ☐ Chronic or acute illnesses
- ☐ Anger

Notes

Symptoms

- [ ] Headache
- [ ] Anger and irritability
- [ ] Backache
- [ ] Arthritis pain
- [ ] Cancer pain
- [ ] Gall stones
- [ ] Bursitis
- [ ] Stomach pain
- [ ] Pain in the calf, especially when walking
- [ ] Facial pain
- [ ] Toothache
- [ ] Gout
- [ ] Many other illnesses

Notes

Action Plan

- [ ] Ice or heat
- [ ] Creams
- [ ] Bandages
- [ ] Soak in an Epsom Salt bath
- [ ] Do creative visualization exercises
- [ ] Massage
- [ ] Medication
- [ ] Gels
- [ ] Rest
- [ ] Doing relaxation exercises
- [ ] Deep breathing
- [ ] Light diet

Notes

I hope that you have found value in this book, and I hope that you will get well and stay well for longer periods.

I would be very grateful if you would leave a review on Amazon. Reviews are valuable to an author. They help other people decide whether or not they would like to read the book.

Thanks so much.

My Books

NON FICTION

How to Live with Bipolar

Bipolar 1 Disorder Rescue Plan

37 Symptoms of Bipolar Depression

The Bipolar Guide

A Practical Guide to Overcoming Loneliness

Get Well and Stay Well with Bipolar Disorder

Life Lessons

FICTION

Shards of Glass Series

Shards of Glass

Fragments of the Past

Memories Lost in Time

SHORT STORIES

One Summer

The Lucky Lady

POETRY

We Never Did Mornings

HUMOR

Funny Old Folk

Author Bio

Sally Alter is a prolific writer who has had bipolar disorder for over fifty years. She is also a Registered Nurse. After writing over 5,000 answers on the popular question and answer website Quora – 800 on bipolar alone – she realized her knowledge, compiled and condensed into books, could really help people.

Sally published her first book, *"How to Live with Bipolar"* at 73 and has gone on to publish four more books on bipolar - *"Bipolar 1 Disorder Rescue Plan," "37 Symptoms of Bipolar Depression," "The Bipolar Guide,"* and *"Get Well and Stay Well."* Helping people and their families and friends through the stress and strain of bipolar has become her mission.

Sally is from London and now lives in Texas. She has traveled all over America in an RV and visited many European countries. When she is not writing, she can be found creating stunning oil paintings, doing colored pencil drawings, reading, completing jigsaw puzzles and spending time with Greta, her beloved cat.

Sally hopes her writing will fill in the gaps left by other bipolar disorder books to help people live more fulfilling lives.

For your **FREE** Bipolar Checklist visit:

Website:
https://sallyalter.com

Or contact me here:

Facebook author page:
https://www.facebook.com/SallyAlterWriter/

Email address:
mandala913@omniglobal.net

www.ingramcontent.com/pod-product-compliance
Lightning Source LLC
LaVergne TN
LVHW022054200926
848481LV00003B/902
* 9 7 9 8 3 4 9 4 4 3 6 2 6 *